Web Audio API

Boris Smus

Beijing · Cambridge · Farnham · Köln · Sebastopol · Tokyo

Web Audio API

by Boris Smus

Printed in the United States of America.

Published by O'Reilly Media, Inc., 1005 Gravenstein Highway North, Sebastopol, CA 95472.

O'Reilly books may be purchased for educational, business, or sales promotional use. Online editions are also available for most titles (*http://my.safaribooksonline.com*). For more information, contact our corporate/institutional sales department: 800-998-9938 or *corporate@oreilly.com*.

Editors: Simon St. Laurent and Meghan Blanchette	**Cover Designer:** Randy Comer
Production Editor: Kara Ebrahim	**Interior Designer:** David Futato
Proofreader: Jilly Gagnon	**Illustrator:** Rebecca Demarest

March 2013:   First Edition

Revision History for the First Edition:

2013-03-07:   First release

See *http://oreilly.com/catalog/errata.csp?isbn=9781449332686* for release details.

ISBN: 978-1-449-33268-6

[LSI]

To my parents: thank you for the music

Table of Contents

Preface

Thank you for picking up the first book on the topic of the Web Audio API. When I first learned of the Web Audio API, I was a complete digital-audio novice embarking on a journey to learn and understand the API, as well as the underlying fundamental audio concepts. This book is what I wish existed when I started experimenting with the API in 2011. It is intended to be a springboard for web developers like I was, with little to no digital-audio expertise. It contains the things I learned from about a year of studying digital audio processing, having conversations with audio experts, and experimenting with the API.

The theoretical bits will be filled in through asides, which will explain the concepts. If you are a digital-audio guru, feel free to skip these. The practical bits will be illustrated with code snippets to give you a better sense of how the API works in real life. Many of the examples also include links to working samples that can be found on this Web Audio API site (*http://webaudioapi.com/samples*).

Structure of This Book

This book aims to give a high-level overview of a number of important features of the Web Audio API, but is not an exhaustive survey of every available feature. It is not intended as a comprehensive guide, but as an easy starting point. Most sections of the book start off by describing an application, outlining the problem and solution, and then showing relevant sample JavaScript Web Audio API code. Interspersed theory sections explain some of the underlying audio concepts in more general terms. The book is structured in the following way:

1. Chapter 1, *Fundamentals* covers the basics of audio graphs, typical graph configurations, audio nodes inside those graphs, loading sound files, and playing sounds back.

2. Chapter 2, *Perfect Timing and Latency* delves into precise scheduling of sound in the future, multiple simultaneous sounds, changing parameters directly or over time, and crossfading.

3. Chapter 3, *Volume and Loudness* covers gain, volume, and loudness, as well as preventing clipping via metering and dynamics compression.

4. Chapter 4, *Pitch and the Frequency Domain* is all about sound frequency, an important property of periodic sound. We'll also talk about oscillators and examining sound in the frequency domain.

5. Chapter 5, *Analysis and Visualization* builds on the earlier chapters to dive into more advanced topics, including biquad filters, simulating acoustic environments, and spatialized sounds.

6. In Chapter 6, *Advanced Topics*, we will take a break from synthesizing and manipulating sound, and analyze and visualize sound instead.

7. Chapter 7, *Integrating with Other Technologies* talks about interfacing Web Audio API with other web APIs like WebRTC and the `<audio>` tag.

The source code of the book itself is released under the Creative Commons license and is available on GitHub (*https://github.com/borismus/webaudioapi.com*).

Conventions Used in This Book

The following typographical conventions are used in this book:

Italic
> Indicates new terms, URLs, email addresses, filenames, and file extensions.

`Constant width`
> Used for program listings, as well as within paragraphs to refer to program elements such as variable or function names, databases, data types, environment variables, statements, and keywords.

`Constant width bold`
> Shows commands or other text that should be typed literally by the user.

`Constant width italic`
> Shows text that should be replaced with user-supplied values or by values determined by context.

 This icon signifies a tip, suggestion, or general note.

This icon indicates a warning or caution.

Using Code Examples

This book is here to help you get your job done. In general, if this book includes code examples, you may use the code in your programs and documentation. You do not need to contact us for permission unless you're reproducing a significant portion of the code. For example, writing a program that uses several chunks of code from this book does not require permission. Selling or distributing a CD-ROM of examples from O'Reilly books does require permission. Answering a question by citing this book and quoting example code does not require permission. Incorporating a significant amount of example code from this book into your product's documentation does require permission.

We appreciate, but do not require, attribution. An attribution usually includes the title, author, publisher, and ISBN. For example: "*Web Audio API* by Boris Smus (O'Reilly). Copyright 2013 Boris Smus, 978-1-449-33268-6."

If you feel your use of code examples falls outside fair use or the permission given above, feel free to contact us at *permissions@oreilly.com*.

Safari® Books Online

 Safari Books Online (*www.safaribooksonline.com*) is an on-demand digital library that delivers expert content in both book and video form from the world's leading authors in technology and business.

Technology professionals, software developers, web designers, and business and creative professionals use Safari Books Online as their primary resource for research, problem solving, learning, and certification training.

Safari Books Online offers a range of product mixes and pricing programs for organizations, government agencies, and individuals. Subscribers have access to thousands of books, training videos, and prepublication manuscripts in one fully searchable database from publishers like O'Reilly Media, Prentice Hall Professional, Addison-Wesley Professional, Microsoft Press, Sams, Que, Peachpit Press, Focal Press, Cisco Press, John Wiley & Sons, Syngress, Morgan Kaufmann, IBM Redbooks, Packt, Adobe Press, FT Press, Apress, Manning, New Riders, McGraw-Hill, Jones & Bartlett, Course Technology, and dozens more. For more information about Safari Books Online, please visit us online.

How to Contact Us

Please address comments and questions concerning this book to the publisher:

O'Reilly Media, Inc.
1005 Gravenstein Highway North
Sebastopol, CA 95472
800-998-9938 (in the United States or Canada)
707-829-0515 (international or local)
707-829-0104 (fax)

We have a web page for this book, where we list errata, examples, and any additional information. You can access this page at *http://oreil.ly/web-audio-api*.

To comment or ask technical questions about this book, send email to *bookques tions@oreilly.com*.

For more information about our books, courses, conferences, and news, see our website at *http://www.oreilly.com*.

Find us on Facebook: *http://facebook.com/oreilly*

Follow us on Twitter: *http://twitter.com/oreillymedia*

Watch us on YouTube: *http://www.youtube.com/oreillymedia*

Thanks!

I am not an expert in digital signals processing, mastering, or mixing by any stretch. I am a software engineer and amateur musician with enough interest in digital audio to spend some time exploring the Web Audio API and wrapping my head around some of its important concepts. To write this book, I had to continually bug others with far more digital-audio experience than me. I'd like to thank them for answering my questions, providing technical reviews for this book, and encouraging me along the way.

Specifically, this book could not have been written without the generous mentorship of Chris Rogers, the primary author of the Web Audio specification and also its main WebKit/Chrome implementer. I owe many thanks to Chris Wilson, who gave an incredibly thorough technical review of this book's content, and to Mark Goldstein, who spent a few late nights doing editorial passes. My thanks to Kevin Ennis for donating webaudioapi.com for hosting samples related to the book. Last but not least, I would have never written this book without the support and interest of a vibrant Web Audio API community on the Web.

Without further ado, let's dive in!

CHAPTER 1

Fundamentals

This chapter will describe how to get started with the Web Audio API, which browsers are supported, how to detect if the API is available, what an audio graph is, what audio nodes are, how to connect nodes together, some basic node types, and finally, how to load sound files and playback sounds.

A Brief History of Audio on the Web

The first way of playing back sounds on the web was via the <bgsound> tag, which let website authors automatically play background music when a visitor opened their pages. This feature was only available in Internet Explorer, and was never standardized or picked up by other browsers. Netscape implemented a similar feature with the <embed> tag, providing basically equivalent functionality.

Flash was the first cross-browser way of playing back audio on the Web, but it had the significant drawback of requiring a plug-in to run. More recently, browser vendors have rallied around the HTML5 <audio> element, which provides native support for audio playback in all modern browsers.

Although audio on the Web no longer requires a plug-in, the <audio> tag has significant limitations for implementing sophisticated games and interactive applications. The following are just some of the limitations of the <audio> element:

- No precise timing controls
- Very low limit for the number of sounds played at once
- No way to reliably pre-buffer a sound
- No ability to apply real-time effects
- No way to analyze sounds

There have been several attempts to create a powerful audio API on the Web to address some of the limitations I previously described. One notable example is the Audio Data API that was designed and prototyped in Mozilla Firefox. Mozilla's approach started with an <audio> element and extended its JavaScript API with additional features. This API has a limited audio graph (more on this later in "The Audio Context" (page 3)), and hasn't been adopted beyond its first implementation. It is currently deprecated in Firefox in favor of the Web Audio API.

In contrast with the Audio Data API, the Web Audio API is a brand new model, completely separate from the <audio> tag, although there are integration points with other web APIs (see Chapter 7). It is a high-level JavaScript API for processing and synthesizing audio in web applications. The goal of this API is to include capabilities found in modern game engines and some of the mixing, processing, and filtering tasks that are found in modern desktop audio production applications. The result is a versatile API that can be used in a variety of audio-related tasks, from games, to interactive applications, to very advanced music synthesis applications and visualizations.

Games and Interactivity

Audio is a huge part of what makes interactive experiences so compelling. If you don't believe me, try watching a movie with the volume muted.

Games are no exception! My fondest video game memories are of the music and sound effects. Now, nearly two decades after the release of some of my favorites, I still can't get Koji Kondo's *Zelda* and Matt Uelmen's *Diablo* soundtracks out of my head. Even the sound effects from these masterfully-designed games are instantly recognizable, from the unit click responses in Blizzard's *Warcraft* and *Starcraft* series to samples from Nintendo's classics.

Sound effects matter a great deal outside of games, too. They have been around in user interfaces (UIs) since the days of the command line, where certain kinds of errors would result in an audible beep. The same idea continues through modern UIs, where well-placed sounds are critical for notifications, chimes, and of course audio and video communication applications like Skype. Assistant software such as Google Now and Siri provide rich, audio-based feedback. As we delve further into a world of ubiquitous computing, speech- and gesture-based interfaces that lend themselves to screen-free interactions are increasingly reliant on audio feedback. Finally, for visually impaired computer users, audio cues, speech synthesis, and speech recognition are critically important to create a usable experience.

Interactive audio presents some interesting challenges. To create convincing in-game music, designers need to adjust to all the potentially unpredictable game states a player can find herself in. In practice, sections of the game can go on for an unknown duration, and sounds can interact with the environment and mix in complex ways, requiring

---

environment-specific effects and relative sound positioning. Finally, there can be a large number of sounds playing at once, all of which need to sound good together and render without introducing quality and performance penalties.

The Audio Context

The Web Audio API is built around the concept of an audio context. The audio context is a directed graph of audio nodes that defines how the audio stream flows from its source (often an audio file) to its destination (often your speakers). As audio passes through each node, its properties can be modified or inspected. The simplest audio context is a connection directly form a source node to a destination node (Figure 1-1).

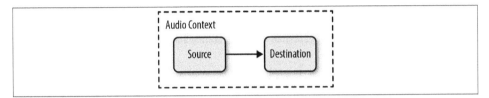

Figure 1-1. The simplest audio context

An audio context can be complex, containing many nodes between the source and destination (Figure 1-2) to perform arbitrarily advanced synthesis or analysis.

Figures 1-1 and 1-2 show audio nodes as blocks. The arrows represent connections between nodes. Nodes can often have multiple incoming and outgoing connections. By default, if there are multiple incoming connections into a node, the Web Audio API simply blends the incoming audio signals together.

The concept of an audio node graph is not new, and derives from popular audio frameworks such as Apple's CoreAudio, which has an analogous Audio Processing Graph API (*http://bit.ly/15tPRNM*). The idea itself is even older, originating in the 1960s with early audio environments like Moog modular synthesizer systems (*http://en.wikipe dia.org/wiki/Moog_synthesizer*).

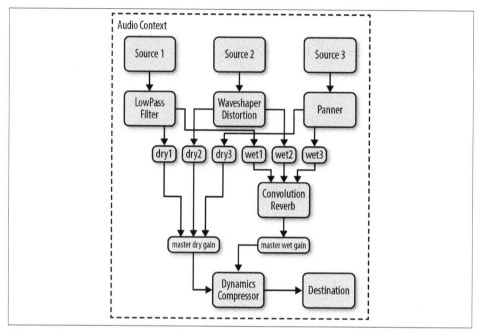

Figure 1-2. A more complex audio context

Initializing an Audio Context

The Web Audio API is currently implemented by the Chrome and Safari browsers (including MobileSafari as of iOS 6) and is available for web developers via JavaScript. In these browsers, the audio context constructor is webkit-prefixed, meaning that instead of creating a new `AudioContext`, you create a new `webkitAudioContext`. However, this will surely change in the future as the API stabilizes enough to ship un-prefixed and as other browser vendors implement it. Mozilla has publicly stated (*https://wiki.mozil la.org/Web_Audio_API*) that they are implementing the Web Audio API in Firefox, and Opera has started participating (*http://lists.w3.org/Archives/Public/public-audio/2012AprJun/0279.html*) in the working group.

With this in mind, here is a liberal way of initializing your audio context that would include other implementations (once they exist):

```
var contextClass = (window.AudioContext ||
  window.webkitAudioContext ||
  window.mozAudioContext ||
  window.oAudioContext ||
  window.msAudioContext);
if (contextClass) {
  // Web Audio API is available.
  var context = new contextClass();
} else {
```

```
    // Web Audio API is not available. Ask the user to use a supported browser.
  }
```

A single audio context can support multiple sound inputs and complex audio graphs, so generally speaking, we will only need one for each audio application we create. The audio context instance includes many methods for creating audio nodes and manipulating global audio preferences. Luckily, these methods are not webkit-prefixed and are relatively stable. The API is still changing, though, so be aware of breaking changes (see Appendix A).

Types of Web Audio Nodes

One of the main uses of audio contexts is to create new audio nodes. Broadly speaking, there are several kinds of audio nodes:

Source nodes
> Sound sources such as audio buffers, live audio inputs, `<audio>` tags, oscillators, and JS processors

Modification nodes
> Filters, convolvers, panners, JS processors, etc.

Analysis nodes
> Analyzers and JS processors

Destination nodes
> Audio outputs and offline processing buffers

Sources need not be based on sound files, but can instead be real-time input from a live instrument or microphone, redirection of the audio output from an audio element [see "Setting Up Background Music with the <audio> Tag" (page 53)], or entirely synthesized sound [see "Audio Processing with JavaScript" (page 51)]. Though the final destination-node is often the speakers, you can also process without sound playback (for example, if you want to do pure visualization) or do offline processing, which results in the audio stream being written to a destination buffer for later use.

Connecting the Audio Graph

Any audio node's output can be connected to any other audio node's input by using the `connect()` function. In the following example, we connect a source node's output into a gain node, and connect the gain node's output into the context's destination:

```
// Create the source.
var source = context.createBufferSource();
// Create the gain node.
var gain = context.createGain();
// Connect source to filter, filter to destination.
```

```
source.connect(gain);
gain.connect(context.destination);
```

Note that `context.destination` is a special node that is associated with the default audio output of your system. The resulting audio graph of the previous code looks like Figure 1-3.

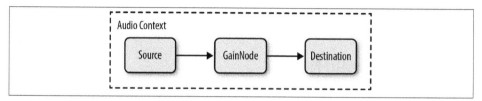

Figure 1-3. Our first audio graph

Once we have connected up a graph like this we can dynamically change it. We can disconnect audio nodes from the graph by calling `node.disconnect(outputNumber)`. For example, to reroute a direct connection between source and destination, circumventing the intermediate node, we can do the following:

```
source.disconnect(0);
gain.disconnect(0);
source.connect(context.destination);
```

Power of Modular Routing

In many games, multiple sources of sound are combined to create the final mix. Sources include background music, game sound effects, UI feedback sounds, and in a multi-player setting, voice chat from other players. An important feature of the Web Audio API is that it lets you separate all of these different channels and gives you full control over each one, or all of them together. The audio graph for such a setup might look like Figure 1-4.

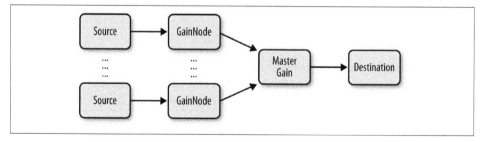

Figure 1-4. Multiple sources with individual gain control as well as a master gain

We have associated a separate gain node with each of the channels and also created a master gain node to control them all. With this setup, it is easy for your players to control the level of each channel separately, precisely the way they want to. For example, many people prefer to play games with the background music turned off.

CRITICAL THEORY

What Is Sound?

In terms of physics, sound is a longitudinal wave (sometimes called a pressure wave) that travels through air or another medium. The source of the sound causes molecules in the air to vibrate and collide with one another. This causes regions of high and low pressure, which come together and fall apart in bands. If you could freeze time and look at the pattern of a sound wave, you might see something like Figure 1-5.

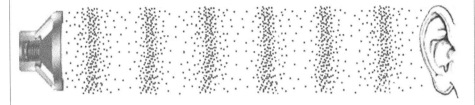

Figure 1-5. A sound pressure wave traveling through air particles

Mathematically, sound can be represented as a function, which ranges over pressure values across the domain of time. Figure 1-6 shows a graph of such a function. You can see that it is analogous to Figure 1-5, with high values corresponding to areas with dense particles (high pressure), and low values corresponding to areas with sparse particles (low pressure).

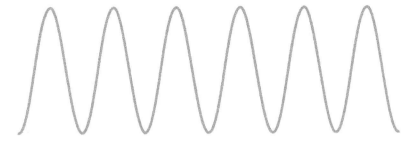

Figure 1-6. A mathematical representation of the sound wave in Figure 1-5

Electronics dating back to the early twentieth century made it possible for us to capture and recreate sounds for the first time. Microphones take the pressure wave and convert it into an electric signal, where (for example) +5 volts corresponds to the highest pressure and −5 volts to the lowest. Conversely, audio speakers take this voltage and convert it back into the pressure waves that we can hear.

Whether we are analyzing sound or synthesizing it, the interesting bits for audio programmers are in the black box in Figure 1-7, tasked with manipulating the audio signal. In the early days of audio, this space was occupied by analog filters and other hardware that would be considered archaic by today's standards. Today, there are modern digital equivalents for many of those old analog pieces of equipment. But before we can use software to tackle the fun stuff, we need to represent sound in a way that computers can work with.

Figure 1-7. Recording and playback

CRITICAL THEORY

What Is Digital Sound?

We can do this by time-sampling the analog signal at some frequency, and encoding the signal at each sample as a number. The rate at which we sample the analog signal is called the *sample rate*. A common sample rate in many sound applications is 44.1 kHz. This means that there are 44,100 numbers recorded for each second of sound. The numbers themselves must fall within some range. There is generally a certain number of bits allocated to each value, which is called the *bit depth*. For most recorded digital audio, including CDs, the bit depth is 16, which is generally enough for most listeners. Audiophiles prefer 24-bit depth, which gives enough precision that people's ears can't hear the difference compared to a higher depth.

The process of converting analog signals into digital ones is called *quantization* (or sampling) and is illustrated in Figure 1-8.

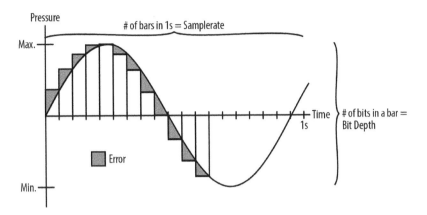

Figure 1-8. Analog sound being quantized, or transformed into digital sound

In Figure 1-8, the quantized digital version isn't quite the same as the analog one because of differences between the bars and the smooth line. The difference (shown in blue) decreases with higher sample rates and bit depths. However, increasing these values also increases the amount of storage required to keep these sounds in memory, on disk, or on the Web. To save space, telephone systems often used sample rates as low as 8 kHz, since the range of frequencies needed to make the human voice intelligible is far smaller than our full audible-frequency range.

By digitizing sound, computers can treat sounds like long arrays of numbers. This sort of encoding is called *pulse-code modulation (PCM)*. Because computers are so good at processing arrays, PCM turns out to be a very powerful primitive for most digital-audio applications. In the Web Audio API world, this long array of numbers representing a sound is abstracted as an AudioBuffer. AudioBuffers can store multiple audio channels (often in stereo, meaning a left and right channel) represented as arrays of floating-point numbers normalized between −1 and 1. The same signal can also be represented as an array of integers, which, in 16-bit, range from (-2^{15}) to $(2^{15} - 1)$.

CRITICAL THEORY

Audio Encoding Formats

Raw audio in PCM format is quite large, which uses extra memory, wastes space on a hard drive, and takes up extra bandwidth when downloaded. Because of this, audio is generally stored in compressed formats. There are two kinds of compression: lossy and lossless. Lossless compression (e.g., FLAC) guarantees that when you compress and then uncompress a sound, the bits are identical. Lossy audio compression (e.g., MP3) exploits features of human hearing to save additional space by throwing out bits that we probably won't be able to hear anyway. Lossy formats are generally good enough for most people, with the exception of some audiophiles.

A commonly used metric for the amount of compression in audio is called *bit rate*, which refers to the number of bits of audio required per second of playback. The higher the bit rate, the more data that can be allocated per unit of time, and thus the less compression required. Often, lossy formats, such as MP3, are described by their bit rate (common rates are 128 and 192 Kb/s). It's possible to encode lossy codecs at arbitrary bit rates. For example, telephone-quality human speech is often compared to 8 Kb/s MP3s. Some formats such as OGG support variable bit rates, where the bit rate changes over time. Be careful not to confuse this concept with sample rate or bit depth [see "What Is Sound?" (page 7)]!

Browser support for different audio formats varies quite a bit. Generally, if the Web Audio API is implemented in a browser, it uses the same loading code that the `<au dio>` tag would, so the browser support matrix for `<audio>` and the Web Audio API is the same. Generally, WAV (which is a simple, lossless, and typically uncompressed format) is supported in all browsers. MP3 is still patent-encumbered, and is therefore not available in some purely open source browsers (e.g., Firefox and Chromium). Unfortunately, the less popular but patent-unencumbered OGG format is still not available in Safari at the time of this writing.

For a more up-to-date roster of audio format support, see *http://mzl.la/13kGelS*.

Loading and Playing Sounds

Web Audio API makes a clear distinction between buffers and source nodes. The idea of this architecture is to decouple the audio asset from the playback state. Taking a record player analogy, buffers are like records and sources are like playheads, except in the Web Audio API world, you can play the same record on any number of playheads simultaneously! Because many applications involve multiple versions of the same buffer playing simultaneously, this pattern is essential. For example, if you want multiple bouncing ball sounds to fire in quick succession, you need to load the bounce buffer only once and schedule multiple sources of playback [see "Multiple Sounds with Variations" (page 32)].

To load an audio sample into the Web Audio API, we can use an `XMLHttpRequest` and process the results with `context.decodeAudioData`. This all happens asynchronously and doesn't block the main UI thread:

```
var request = new XMLHttpRequest();
request.open('GET', url, true);
request.responseType = 'arraybuffer';

// Decode asynchronously
request.onload = function() {
```

```
    context.decodeAudioData(request.response, function(theBuffer) {
      buffer = theBuffer;
    }, onError);
  }
  request.send();
```

Audio buffers are only one possible source of playback. Other sources include direct input from a microphone or line-in device or an <audio> tag among others (see Chapter 7).

Once you've loaded your buffer, you can create a source node (AudioBufferSourceNode) for it, connect the source node into your audio graph, and call start(0) on the source node. To stop a sound, call stop(0) on the source node. Note that both of these function calls require a time in the coordinate system of the current audio context (see Chapter 2):

```
function playSound(buffer) {
  var source = context.createBufferSource();
  source.buffer = buffer;
  source.connect(context.destination);
  source.start(0);
}
```

Games often have background music playing in a loop. However, be careful about being overly repetitive with your selection: if a player is stuck in an area or level, and the same sample continuously plays in the background, it may be worthwhile to gradually fade out the track to prevent frustration. Another strategy is to have mixes of various intensity that gradually crossfade into one another depending on the game situation [see "Gradually Varying Audio Parameters" (page 16)].

Putting It All Together

As you can see from the previous code listings, there's a bit of setup to get sounds playing in the Web Audio API. For a real game, consider implementing a JavaScript abstraction around the Web Audio API. An example of this idea is the following BufferLoader class. It puts everything together into a simple loader, which, given a set of paths, returns a set of audio buffers. Here's how such a class can be used:

```
window.onload = init;
var context;
var bufferLoader;

function init() {
  context = new webkitAudioContext();

  bufferLoader = new BufferLoader(
    context,
    [
      '../sounds/hyper-reality/br-jam-loop.wav',
```

```
            '../sounds/hyper-reality/laughter.wav',
        ],
        finishedLoading
        );

    bufferLoader.load();
}

function finishedLoading(bufferList) {
    // Create two sources and play them both together.
    var source1 = context.createBufferSource();
    var source2 = context.createBufferSource();
    source1.buffer = bufferList[0];
    source2.buffer = bufferList[1];

    source1.connect(context.destination);
    source2.connect(context.destination);
    source1.start(0);
    source2.start(0);
}
```

For a simple reference implementation of BufferLoader, take a look at *http://webau dioapi.com/samples/shared.js.*

CHAPTER 2

Perfect Timing and Latency

One of the strengths of the Web Audio API as compared to the `<audio>` tag is that it comes with a low-latency precise-timing model.

Low latency is very important for games and other interactive applications since you often need fast auditory response to user actions. If the feedback is not immediate, the user will sense the delay, which will lead to frustration. In practice, due to imperfections of human hearing, there is leeway for a delay of up to 20 ms or so, but the number varies depending on many factors.

Precise timing enables you to schedule events at specific times in the future. This is very important for scripted scenes and musical applications.

Timing Model

One of the key things that the audio context provides is a consistent timing model and frame of reference for time. Importantly, this model is different from the one used for JavaScript timers such as `setTimeout`, `setInterval`, and `new Date()`. It is also different from the performance clock provided by `window.performance.now()`.

All of the absolute times that you will be dealing with in the Web Audio API are in seconds (not milliseconds!), in the coordinate system of the specified audio context. The current time can be retrieved from the audio context via the `currentTime` property. Although the units are seconds, time is stored as a floating-point value with high precision.

Precise Playback and Resume

The `start()` function makes it easy to schedule precise sound playback for games and other time-critical applications. To get this working properly, ensure that your sound buffers are pre-loaded [see "Loading and Playing Sounds" (page 10)]. Without a pre-loaded buffer, you will have to wait an unknown amount of time for the browser to fetch the sound file, and then for the Web Audio API to decode it. The failure mode in this case is you want to play a sound at a precise instant, but the buffer is still loading or decoding.

Sounds can be scheduled to play at a precise time by specifying the first (when) parameter of the start() call. This parameter is in the coordinate system of the AudioContext's currentTime. If the parameter is less than the currentTime, it is played immediately. Thus start(0) always plays sound immediately, but to schedule sound in 5 seconds, you would call start(context.currentTime + 5).

Sound buffers can also be played from a specific time offset by specifying a second parameter to the start() call, and limited to a specific duration with a third optional parameter. For example, if we want to pause a sound and play it back from the paused position, we can implement a pause by tracking the amount of time a sound has been playing in the current session and also tracking the last offset in order to resume later:

```
// Assume context is a web audio context, buffer is a pre-loaded audio buffer.
var startOffset = 0;
var startTime = 0;

function pause() {
  source.stop();
  // Measure how much time passed since the last pause.
  startOffset += context.currentTime - startTime;
}
```

Once a source node has finished playing back, it can't play back more. To play back the underlying buffer again, you need to create a new source node (AudioBufferSource Node) and call start():

```
function play() {
  startTime = context.currentTime;
  var source = context.createBufferSource();
  // Connect graph
  source.buffer = this.buffer;
  source.loop = true;
  source.connect(context.destination);
  // Start playback, but make sure we stay in bound of the buffer.
  source.start(0, startOffset % buffer.duration);
}
```

Though recreating the source node may seem inefficient at first, keep in mind that source nodes are heavily optimized for this pattern. Remember that if you keep a handle to the AudioBuffer, you don't need to make another request to the asset to play the same sound again. By having this AudioBuffer around, you have a clean separation between buffer and player, and can easily play back multiple versions of the same buffer overlapping in time. If you find yourself needing to repeat this pattern, encapsulate playback with a simple helper function like playSound(buffer) in an earlier code snippet.

Scheduling Precise Rhythms

The Web Audio API lets developers precisely schedule playback in the future. To demonstrate this, let's set up a simple rhythm track. Probably the simplest and most widely known drumkit pattern is shown in Figure 2-1, in which a hihat is played every eighth note, and the kick and snare are played on alternating quarter notes, in 4/4 time.

Figure 2-1. Sheet music for one of the most basic drum patterns

Assuming we have already loaded the kick, snare, and hihat buffers, the code to do this is simple:

```
for (var bar = 0; bar < 2; bar++) {
  var time = startTime + bar * 8 * eighthNoteTime;
  // Play the bass (kick) drum on beats 1, 5
  playSound(kick, time);
  playSound(kick, time + 4 * eighthNoteTime);

  // Play the snare drum on beats 3, 7
  playSound(snare, time + 2 * eighthNoteTime);
  playSound(snare, time + 6 * eighthNoteTime);

  // Play the hihat every eighth note.
  for (var i = 0; i < 8; ++i) {
    playSound(hihat, time + i * eighthNoteTime);
  }
}
```

Once you've scheduled sound in the future, there is no way to unschedule that future playback event, so if you are dealing with an application that quickly changes, scheduling sounds too far into the future is not advisable. A good way of dealing with this problem is to create your own scheduler using JavaScript timers and an event queue. This approach is described in A Tale of Two Clocks (*http://www.html5rocks.com/en/*).

Demo: to see this code in action, visit http://webaudioapi.com/samples/rhythm/.

Changing Audio Parameters

Many types of audio nodes have configurable parameters. For example, the GainNode has a gain parameter that controls the gain multiplier for all sounds going through the node. Specifically, a gain of 1 does not affect the amplitude, 0.5 halves it, and 2 doubles it [see "Volume, Gain, and Loudness" (page 21)]. Let's set up a graph as follows:

```
// Create a gain node.
var gainNode = context.createGain();
// Connect the source to the gain node.
source.connect(gainNode);
// Connect the gain node to the destination.
gainNode.connect(context.destination);
```

In the context of the API, audio parameters are represented as AudioParam instances. The values of these nodes can be changed directly by setting the value attribute of a param instance:

```
// Reduce the volume.
gainNode.gain.value = 0.5;
```

The values can also be changed later, via precisely scheduled parameter changes in the future. We could also use setTimeout to do this scheduling, but this is not precise for several reasons:

1. Millisecond-based timing may not be enough precision.
2. The main JS thread may be busy with high-priority tasks like page layout, garbage collection, and callbacks from other APIs, which delays timers.
3. The JS timer is affected by tab state. For example, interval timers in backgrounded tabs fire more slowly than if the tab is in the foreground.

Instead of setting the value directly, we can call the setValueAtTime() function, which takes a value and a start time as arguments. For example, the following snippet sets the gain value of a GainNode in one second:

```
gainNode.gain.setValueAtTime(0.5, context.currentTime + 1);
```

Demo: for a simple example of changing the gain parameter, visit http://webaudioa pi.com/samples/volume/.

Gradually Varying Audio Parameters

In many cases, rather than changing a parameter abruptly, you would prefer a more gradual change. For example, when building a music player application, we want to fade the current track out, and fade the new one in, to avoid a jarring transition. While you can achieve this with multiple calls to setValueAtTime as described previously, this is inconvenient.

The Web Audio API provides a convenient set of RampToValue methods to gradually change the value of any parameter. These functions are linearRampToValueAtTime() and exponentialRampToValueAtTime(). The difference between these two lies in the way the transition happens. In some cases, an exponential transition makes more sense, since we perceive many aspects of sound in an exponential manner.

Let's take an example of scheduling a crossfade in the future. Given a playlist, we can transition between tracks by scheduling a gain decrease on the currently playing track, and a gain increase on the next one, both slightly before the current track finishes playing:

```
function createSource(buffer) {
  var source = context.createBufferSource();
  var gainNode = context.createGainNode();
  source.buffer = buffer;
  // Connect source to gain.
  source.connect(gainNode);
  // Connect gain to destination.
  gainNode.connect(context.destination);

  return {
    source: source,
    gainNode: gainNode
  };
}

function playHelper(buffers, iterations, fadeTime) {
  var currTime = context.currentTime;
  for (var i = 0; i < iterations; i++) {
    // For each buffer, schedule its playback in the future.
    for (var j = 0; j < buffers.length; j++) {
      var buffer = buffers[j];
      var duration = buffer.duration;
      var info = createSource(buffer);
      var source = info.source;
      var gainNode = info.gainNode;
      // Fade it in.
      gainNode.gain.linearRampToValueAtTime(0, currTime);
      gainNode.gain.linearRampToValueAtTime(1, currTime + fadeTime);
      // Then fade it out.
      gainNode.gain.linearRampToValueAtTime(1, currTime + duration-fadeTime);
      gainNode.gain.linearRampToValueAtTime(0, currTime + duration);

      // Play the track now.
      source.noteOn(currTime);

      // Increment time for the next iteration.
      currTime += duration - fadeTime;
    }
  }
}
```

Demo: to see this code in action, visit http://webaudioapi.com/samples/crossfade-playlist/.

Custom Timing Curves

If neither a linear nor an exponential curve satisfies your needs, you can also specify your own value curve via an array of values using the setValueCurveAtTime function. With this function, you can define a custom timing curve by providing an array of timing values. It's a shortcut for making a bunch of setValueAtTime calls, and should be used in this case. For example, if we want to create a tremolo effect, we can apply an oscillating curve to the gain AudioParam of a GainNode, as in Figure 2-2.

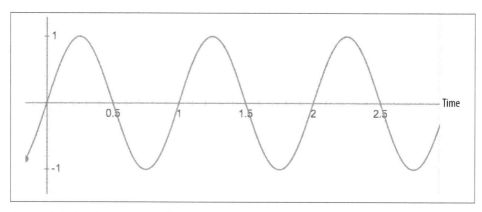

Figure 2-2. A value curve oscillating over time

The oscillating curve in the previous figure could be implemented with the following code:

```
var DURATION = 2;
var FREQUENCY = 1;
var SCALE = 0.4;

// Split the time into valueCount discrete steps.
var valueCount = 4096;
// Create a sinusoidal value curve.
var values = new Float32Array(valueCount);
for (var i = 0; i < valueCount; i++) {
  var percent = (i / valueCount) * DURATION*FREQUENCY;
  values[i] = 1 + (Math.sin(percent * 2*Math.PI) * SCALE);
  // Set the last value to one, to restore playbackRate to normal at the end.
  if (i == valueCount - 1) {
    values[i] = 1;
  }
}
// Apply it to the gain node immediately, and make it last for 2 seconds.
this.gainNode.gain.setValueCurveAtTime(values, context.currentTime, DURATION);
```

In the previous snippet, we've manually computed a sine curve and applied it to the gain parameter to create a tremolo sound effect. It took a bit of math, though.

This brings us to a very nifty feature of the Web Audio API that lets us build effects like tremolo more easily. We can take any audio stream that would ordinarily be connected into another AudioNode, and instead connect it into any AudioParam. This important idea is the basis for many sound effects. The previous code is actually an example of such an effect called a low frequency oscillator (LFO) applied to the gain, which is used to build effects such as vibrato, phasing, and tremolo. By using the oscillator node [see "Oscillator-Based Direct Sound Synthesis" (page 34)], we can easily rebuild the previous example as follows:

```
// Create oscillator.
var osc = context.createOscillator();
osc.frequency.value = FREQUENCY;
var gain = context.createGain();
gain.gain.value = SCALE;
osc.connect(gain);
gain.connect(this.gainNode.gain);

// Start immediately, and stop in 2 seconds.
osc.start(0);
osc.stop(context.currentTime + DURATION);
```

The latter approach is more efficient than creating a custom value curve and saves us from having to compute sine functions manually by creating a loop to repeat the effect.

CHAPTER 3

Volume and Loudness

Once we are ready to play a sound, whether from an `AudioBuffer` or from other sources, one of the most basic parameters we can change is the loudness of the sound.

The main way to affect the loudness of a sound is using `GainNodes`. As previously mentioned, these nodes have a gain parameter, which acts as a multiplier on the incoming sound buffer. The default gain value is one, which means that the input sound is unaffected. Values between zero and one reduce the loudness, and values greater than one amplify the loudness. Negative gain (values less than zero) inverts the waveform (i.e., the amplitude is flipped).

CRITICAL THEORY

Volume, Gain, and Loudness

Let's start with some definitions. *Loudness* is a subjective measure of how intensely our ears perceive a sound. *Volume* is a measure of the physical amplitude of a sound wave. *Gain* is a scale multiplier affecting a sound's amplitude as it is being processed.

In other words, when undergoing a gain, the amplitude of a sound wave is scaled, with the gain value used as a multiplier. For example, while a gain value of one will not affect the sound wave at all, Figure 3-1 illustrates what happens to a sound wave if you send it through a gain factor of two.

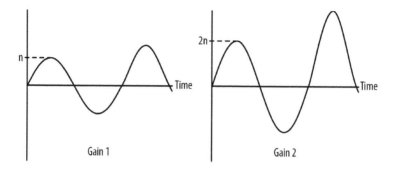

Figure 3-1. Original soundform on the left, gain 2 soundform on the right

Generally speaking, power in a wave is measured in decibels (abbreviated dB), or one tenth of a Bel, named after Alexander Graham Bell. Decibels are a relative, logarithmic unit that compare the level being measured to some reference point. There are many different reference points for measuring dB, and each reference point is indicated with a suffix on the unit. Saying that a signal is some number of dB is meaningless without a reference point! For example, dBV, dBu, and dBm are all useful for measuring electrical signals. Since we are dealing with digital audio, we are mainly concerned with two measures: dBFS and dBSPL.

The first is *dBFS*, or decibels full scale. The highest possible level of sound produced by audio equipment is 0 dBFS. All other levels are expressed in negative numbers.

dBFS is described mathematically as:

```
dBFS = 20 * log( [sample level] / [max level] )
```

The maximum dBFS value in a 16-bit audio system is:

```
max = 20 * log(1111 1111 1111 1111/1111 1111 1111 1111) = log(1) = 0
```

Note that the maximum dBFS value will always be 0 by definition, since log(1) = 0. Similarly, the minimum dBFS value in the same system is:

```
min = 20 * log(0000 0000 0000 0001/1111 1111 1111 1111) = -96 dBFS
```

dBFS is a measure of gain, not volume. You can play a 0-dBFS signal through your stereo with the stereo gain set very low and hardly be able to hear anything. Conversely, you can play a −30-dBFS signal with the stereo gain maxed and blow your eardrums away.

That said, you've probably heard someone describe the volume of a sound in decibels. Technically speaking, they were referring to *dBSPL*, or decibels relative to sound pressure level. Here, the reference point is 0.000002 newtons per square meter (roughly the sound of a mosquito flying 3 m away). There is no upper value to dBSPL, but in practice, we want to stay below levels of ear damage (~120 dBSPL) and well below the threshold of pain (~150 dBSPL). The Web Audio API does not use dBSPL, since the final volume of the sound depends on the OS gain and the speaker gain, and only deals with dBFS.

The logarithmic definition of decibels correlates somewhat to the way our ears perceive loudness, but loudness is still a very subjective concept. Comparing the dB values of a sound and the same sound with a 2x gain, we can see that we've gained about 6 dB:

```
diff = 20 * log(2/2^16) - 20 * log(1/2^16) = 6.02 dB
```

Every time we add 6 dB or so, we actually double the amplitude of the signal. Comparing the sound at a rock concert (~110 dBSPL) to your alarm clock (~80 dBSPL), the difference between the two is (110 − 80)/6 dB, or roughly 5 times louder, with a gain multiplier of $2^5 = 32x$. A volume knob on a stereo is therefore also calibrated to increase the amplitude exponentially. In other words, turning the volume knob by 3 units multiplies the amplitude of the signal roughly by a factor of 2^3 or 8 times. In practice, the exponential model described here is merely an approximation to the way our ears perceive loudness, and audio equipment manufacturers often have their own custom gain curves that are neither linear nor exponential.

Equal Power Crossfading

Often in a game setting, you have a situation where you want to crossfade between two environments that have different sounds associated with them. However, when to crossfade and by how much is not known in advance; perhaps it varies with the position of the game avatar, which is controlled by the player. In this case, we cannot do an automatic ramp.

In general, doing a straightforward, linear fade will result in the following graph. It can sound unbalanced because of a volume dip between the two samples, as shown in Figure 3-2.

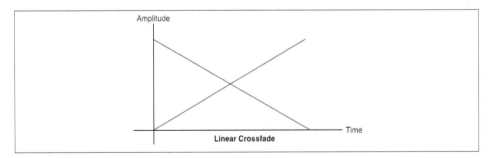

Figure 3-2. A linear crossfade between two tracks

To address this issue, we use an equal power curve, in which the corresponding gain curves are neither linear nor exponential, and intersect at a higher amplitude (Figure 3-3). This helps avoid a dip in volume in the middle part of the crossfade, when both sounds are mixed together equally.

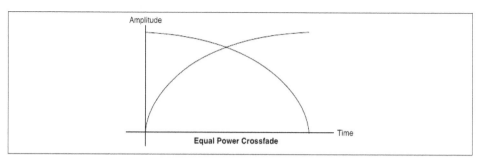

Figure 3-3. An equal power crossfade sounds much better

The graph in Figure 3-3 can be generated with a bit of math:

```
function equalPowerCrossfade(percent) {
  // Use an equal-power crossfading curve:
  var gain1 = Math.cos(percent * 0.5*Math.PI);
  var gain2 = Math.cos((1.0 - percent) * 0.5*Math.PI);
  this.ctl1.gainNode.gain.value = gain1;
  this.ctl2.gainNode.gain.value = gain2;
}
```

Demo: to listen to an equal power crossfade, visit http://webaudioapi.com/samples/cross fade/.

CRITICAL THEORY

Clipping and Metering

Like images exceeding the boundaries of a canvas, sounds can also be clipped if the waveform exceeds its maximum level. The distinct distortion that this produces is obviously undesirable. Audio equipment often has indicators that show the magnitude of audio levels to help engineers and listeners produce output that does not clip. These indicators are called meters (Figure 3-4) and often have a green zone (no clipping), yellow zone (close to clipping), and red zone (clipping).

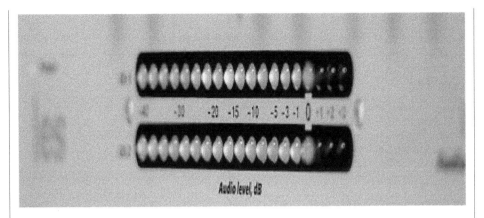

Figure 3-4. A meter in a typical receiver

Clipped sound looks bad on a monitor and sounds no better. It's important to listen for harsh distortions, or conversely, overly subdued mixes that force your listeners to crank up the volume. If you're in either of these situations, read on!

Using Meters to Detect and Prevent Clipping

Since multiple sounds playing simultaneously are additive with no level reduction, you may find yourself in a situation where you are exceeding past the threshold of your speaker's capability. The maximum level of sound is 0 dBFS, or 2^{16}, for 16-bit audio. In the floating point version of the signal, these bit values are mapped to $[-1, 1]$. The waveform of a sound that's being clipped looks something like Figure 3-5. In the context of the Web Audio API, sounds clip if the values sent to the destination node lie outside of the range. It's a good idea to leave some room (called *headroom*) in your final mix so that you aren't too close to the clipping threshold.

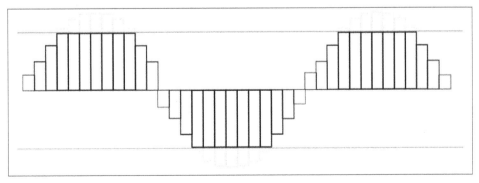

Figure 3-5. A diagram of a waveform being clipped

In addition to close listening, you can check whether or not you are clipping your sound programmatically by putting a script processor node into your audio graph. Clipping may occur if any of the PCM values are out of the acceptable range. In this sample, we check both left and right channels for clipping, and if clipping is detected, save the last clipping time:

```
function onProcess(e) {
  var leftBuffer = e.inputBuffer.getChannelData(0);
  var rightBuffer = e.inputBuffer.getChannelData(1);
  checkClipping(leftBuffer);
  checkClipping(rightBuffer);
}

function checkClipping(buffer) {
  var isClipping = false;
  // Iterate through buffer to check if any of the |values| exceeds 1.
  for (var i = 0; i < buffer.length; i++) {
    var absValue = Math.abs(buffer[i]);
    if (absValue >= 1.0) {
      isClipping = true;
      break;
    }
  }
  this.isClipping = isClipping;
  if (isClipping) {
    lastClipTime = new Date();
  }
}
```

An alternative implementation of metering could poll a real-time analyzer in the audio graph for getFloatFrequencyData at render time, as determined by requestAnima tionFrame (see Chapter 5). This approach is more efficient, but misses a lot of the signal (including places where it potentially clips), since rendering happens most at 60 times a second, whereas the audio signal changes far more quickly.

The way to prevent clipping is to reduce the overall level of the signal. If you are clipping, apply some fractional gain on a master audio gain node to subdue your mix to a level that prevents clipping. In general, you should tweak gains to anticipate the worst case, but getting this right is more of an art than a science. In practice, since the sounds playing in your game or interactive application may depend on a huge variety of factors that are decided at runtime, it can be difficult to pick the master gain value that prevents clipping in all cases. For this unpredictable case, look to dynamics compression, which is discussed in "Dynamics Compression" (page 28).

Demo: for an example of a very simple meter, visit http://webaudioapi.com/samples/metering/.

Understanding Dynamic Range

In audio, *dynamic range* refers to the difference between the loudest and quietest parts of a sound. The amount of dynamic range in musical pieces varies greatly depending on genre. Classical music has large dynamic range and often features very quiet sections followed by relatively loud ones. Many popular genres like rock and electronica tend to have a small dynamic range, and are uniformly loud because of an apparent competition (known pejoratively as the "Loudness War") to increase the loudness of tracks to meet consumer demands. This uniform loudness is generally achieved by using dynamic range compression.

That said, there are many legitimate uses of compression. Sometimes recorded music has such a large dynamic range that there are sections that sound so quiet or loud that the listener constantly needs to have a finger on the volume knob. Compression can quiet down the loud parts while making the quiet parts audible. Figure 3-6 illustrates a waveform (above), and then the same waveform with compression applied (below). You can see that the sound is louder overall, and there is less variance in the amplitude.

Figure 3-6. The effects of dynamics compression

For games and interactive applications, you may not know beforehand what your sound output will look like. Because of games' dynamic nature, you may have very quiet periods (e.g., stealthy sneaking) followed by very loud ones (e.g., a warzone). A compressor node can be helpful in suddenly loud situations for reducing the likelihood of clipping [see "Clipping and Metering" (page 24)].

Compressors can be modeled with a compression curve with several parameters, all of which can be tweaked with the Web Audio API. Two of the main parameters of a compressor are threshold and ratio. Threshold refers to the lowest volume at which a compressor starts reducing dynamic range. Ratio determines how much gain reduction is applied by the compressor. Figure 3-7 illustrates the effect of threshold and various compression ratios on the compression curve.

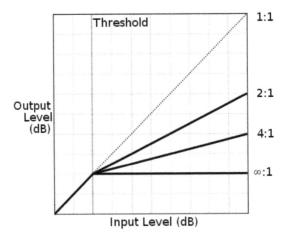

Figure 3-7. A sample compression curve with basic parameters

Dynamics Compression

Compressors are available in the Web Audio API as DynamicsCompressorNodes. Using moderate amounts of dynamics compression in your mix is generally a good idea, especially in a game setting where, as previously discussed, you don't know exactly what sounds will play and when. One case where compression should be avoided is when dealing with painstakingly mastered tracks that have been tuned to sound "just right" already, which are not being mixed with any other tracks.

Implementing dynamic compression in the Web Audio API is simply a matter of including a dynamics compressor node in your audio graph, generally as the last node before the destination:

```
var compressor = context.createDynamicsCompressor();
mix.connect(compressor);
compressor.connect(context.destination);
```

The node can be configured with some additional parameters as described in the theory section, but the defaults are quite good for most purposes. For more information about configuring the compression curve, see the Web Audio API specification (*https://dvcs.w3.org/hg/audio/raw-file/tip/webaudio/specification.html*).

CHAPTER 4

Pitch and the Frequency Domain

So far we have learned about some basic properties of sound: timing and volume. To do more complex things, such as sound equalization (e.g., increasing the bass and decreasing the treble), we need more complex tools. This section explains some of the tools that allow you to do these more interesting transformations, which include the ability to simulate different sorts of environments and manipulate sounds directly with JavaScript.

CRITICAL THEORY

Basics of Musical Pitch

Music consists of many sounds played simultaneously. Sounds produced by musical instruments can be very complex, as the sound bounces through various parts of the instrument and is shaped in unique ways. However, these musical tones all have one thing in common: physically, they are periodic waveforms. This periodicity is perceived by our ears as pitch. The pitch of a note is measured in frequency, or the number of times the wave pattern repeats every second, specified in *hertz*. The frequency is the time (in seconds) between the crests of the wave. As illustrated in Figure 4-1, if we halve the wave in the time dimension, we end up with a correspondingly doubled frequency, which sounds to our ears like the same tone, one octave higher. Conversely, if we extend the wave's frequency by two, this brings the tone an octave down. Thus, pitch (like volume) is perceived exponentially by our ears: at every octave, the frequency doubles.

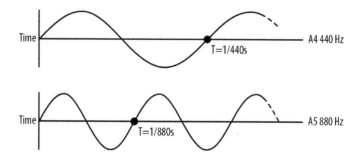

Figure 4-1. Graph of perfect A4 and A5 tones side by side

Octaves are split up into 12 semitones. Each adjacent semitone pair has an identical frequency ratio (at least in equal-tempered tunings). In other words, the ratios of the frequencies of A4 to A#4 are identical to A#4 to B.

Figure 4-1 shows how we would derive the ratio between every successive semitone, given that:

1. To transpose a note up an octave, we double the frequency of the note.
2. Each octave is split up into 12 semitones, which, in an equal tempered tuning, have identical frequency ratios.

Let's define a f_0 to be some frequency, and f_1 to be that same note one octave higher. we know that this is the relationship between them:

$$f_1 = 2 * f_0$$

Next, let k be the fixed multiplier between any two adjacent semitones. Since there are 12 semitones in an octave, we also know the following:

$$f_1 = f_0 * k * k * k * ... * k(12x) = f_0 * k^{12}$$

Solving the system of equations above, we have the following:

$$2 * f_0 = f_0 * k^{12}$$

Solving for k:

$$k = 2^{(1/12)} = 1.0595...$$

Conveniently, all of this semitone-related offsetting isn't really necessary to do manually, since many audio environments (the Web Audio API included) include a notion of detune, which linearizes the frequency domain. Detune is measured in *cents*, with each octave consisting of 1200 cents, and each semitone consisting of 100 cents. By specifying a detune of 1200, you move up an octave. Specifying a detune of −1200 moves you down an octave.

Pitch and playbackRate

The Web Audio API provides a `playbackRate` parameter on each `AudioSourceNode`. This value can be set to affect the pitch of any sound buffer. Note that the pitch as well as the duration of the sample will be affected in this case. There are sophisticated methods that try to affect pitch independent of duration, but this is quite difficult to do in a general-purpose way without introducing blips, scratches, and other undesirable artifacts to the mix.

As discussed in "Basics of Musical Pitch" (page 29), to compute the frequencies of successive semitones, we simply multiply the frequency by the semitone ratio $2^{1/12}$. This is very useful if you are developing a musical instrument or using pitch for randomization in a game setting. The following code plays a tone at a given frequency offset in semitones:

```
function playNote(semitones) {
  // Assume a new source was created from a buffer.
  var semitoneRatio = Math.pow(2, 1/12);
  source.playbackRate.value = Math.pow(semitoneRatio, semitones);
  source.start(0);
}
```

As we discussed earlier, our ears perceive pitch exponentially. Treating pitch as an exponential quantity can be inconvenient, since we often deal with awkward values such as the twelfth root of two. Instead of doing that, we can use the detune parameter to specify our offset in cents. Thus you can rewrite the above function using detune in an easier way:

```
function playNote(semitones) {
  // Assume a new source was created from a buffer.
  source.detune.value = semitones * 100;
  source.start(0);
}
```

If you pitch shift by too many semitones (e.g., by calling `playNote(24);`), you will start to hear distortions. Because of this, digital pianos include multiple samples for each instrument. Good digital pianos avoid pitch bending at all, and include a separate sample recorded specifically for each key. Great digital pianos often include multiple samples for each key, which are played back depending on the velocity of the key press.

Multiple Sounds with Variations

A key feature of sound effects in games is that there can be many of them simultaneously. Imagine you're in the middle of a gunfight with multiple actors shooting machine guns. Each machine gun fires many times per second, causing tens of sound effects to be played at the same time. Playing back sound from multiple, precisely-timed sources simultaneously is one place the Web Audio API really shines.

Now, if all of the machine guns in your game sounded exactly the same, that would be pretty boring. Of course the sound would vary based on distance from the target and relative position [more on this later in "Spatialized Sound" (page 49)], but even that might not be enough. Luckily the Web Audio API provides a way to easily tweak the previous example in at least two simple ways:

1. With a subtle shift in time between bullets firing
2. By changing pitch to better simulate the randomness of the real world

Using our knowledge of timing and pitch, implementing these two effects is pretty straightforward:

```
function shootRound(numberOfRounds, timeBetweenRounds) {
  var time = context.currentTime;
  // Make multiple sources using the same buffer and play in quick succession.
  for (var i = 0; i < numberOfRounds; i++) {
    var source = this.makeSource(bulletBuffer);
    source.playbackRate.value = 1 + Math.random() * RANDOM_PLAYBACK;
    source.start(time + i * timeBetweenRounds + Math.random() * RANDOM_VOLUME);
  }
}
```

The Web Audio API automatically merges multiple sounds playing at once, essentially just adding the waveforms together. This can cause problems such as clipping, which we discuss in "Clipping and Metering" (page 24).

This example adds some variety to `AudioBuffers` loaded from sound files. In some cases, it is desirable to have fully synthesized sound effects and no buffers at all [see "Procedurally Generated Sound" (page 45)].

Demo: to hear multiple gunshot samples played in rapid succession, visit http://webaudioapi.com/samples/rapid-sounds/.

CRITICAL THEORY

Understanding the Frequency Domain

So far in our theoretical excursions, we've only examined sound as a function of pressure as it varies over time. Another useful way of looking at sound is to plot amplitude and

---

see how it varies over frequency. This results in graphs where the domain (x-axis) is in units of frequency (Hz). Graphs of sound plotted this way are said to be in the *frequency domain*.

The relationship between the time-domain and frequency-domain graphs is based on the idea of *fourier decomposition*. As we saw earlier, sound waves are often cyclical in nature. Mathematically, periodic sound waves can be seen as the sum of multiple simple sine waves of different frequency and amplitude. The more such sine waves we add together, the better an approximation of the original function we can get. We can take a signal and find its component sine waves by applying a fourier transformation, the details of which are outside the scope of this book. Many algorithms exist to get this decomposition too, the best known of which is the Fast Fourier Transform (FFT). Luckily, the Web Audio API comes with an implementation of this algorithm. We will discuss how it works later [see "Frequency Analysis" (page 37)].

In general, we can take a sound wave, figure out the constituent sine wave breakdown, and plot the (frequency, amplitude) as points on a new graph to get a frequency domain plot. Figure 4-2 shows a pure A note at 440 Hz (called A4).

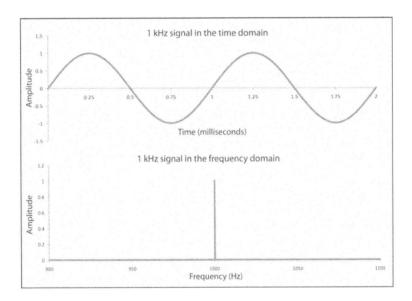

Figure 4-2. A perfectly sinusoidal 1-KHz sound wave represented in both time and frequency domains

Looking at the frequency domain can give a better sense of the qualities of the sound, including pitch content, amount of noise, and much more. Advanced algorithms like pitch detection can be built on top of the frequency domain. Sound produced by real musical instruments have overtones, so an A4 played by a piano has a frequency domain plot that looks (and sounds) very different from the same A4 pitch played by a trumpet.

Regardless of the complexity of sounds, the same fourier decomposition ideas apply. Figure 4-3 shows a more complex fragment of a sound in both the time and frequency domains.

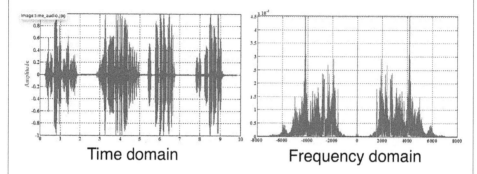

Figure 4-3. A complex sound wave shown in both time and frequency domains

These graphs behave quite differently over time. If you were to very slowly play back the sound in Figure 4-3 and observe it moving along each graph, you would notice the time domain graph (on the left) progressing left to right. The frequency domain graph (on the right) is the frequency analysis of the waveform at a moment in time, so it might change more quickly and less predictably.

Importantly, frequency-domain analysis is still useful when the sound examined is not perceived as having a specific pitch. Wind, percussive sources, and gunshots have distinct representations in the frequency domain. For example, white noise has a flat frequency domain spectrum, since each frequency is equally represented.

Oscillator-Based Direct Sound Synthesis

As we discussed early in this book, digital sound in the Web Audio API is represented as an array of floats in AudioBuffers. Most of the time, the buffer is created by loading a sound file, or on the fly from some sound stream. In some cases, we might want to synthesize our own sounds. We can do this by creating audio buffers programmatically using JavaScript, which simply evaluate a mathematical function at regular periods and assign values to an array. By taking this approach, we can manually change the amplitude and frequency of our sine wave, or even concatenate multiple sine waves together to create arbitrary sounds [recall the principles of fourier transformations from "Understanding the Frequency Domain" (page 32)].

Though possible, doing this work in JavaScript is inefficient and complex. Instead, the Web Audio API provides primitives that let you do this with oscillators: Oscillator Node. These nodes have configurable frequency and detune [see the "Basics of Musical

Pitch" (page 29)]. They also have a type that represents the kind of wave to generate. Built-in types include the sine, triangle, sawtooth, and square waves, as shown in Figure 4-4.

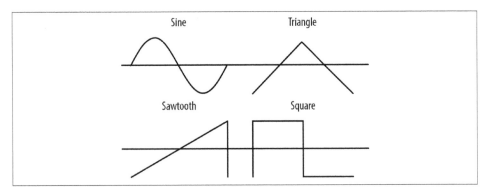

Figure 4-4. Types of basic soundwave shapes that the oscillator can generate

Oscillators can easily be used in audio graphs in place of AudioBufferSourceNodes. An example of this follows:

```
function play(semitone) {
    // Create some sweet sweet nodes.
    var oscillator = context.createOscillator();
    oscillator.connect(context.destination);
    // Play a sine type curve at A4 frequency (440hz).
    oscillator.frequency.value = 440;
    oscillator.detune.value = semitone * 100;
    // Note: this constant will be replaced with "sine".
    oscillator.type = oscillator.SINE;
    oscillator.start(0);
}
```

Demo: to listen to oscillators of various types, visit http://webaudioapi.com/samples/oscillator/.

In addition to these basic wave types, you can create a custom wave table for your oscillator by using harmonic tables. This lets you efficiently create wave shapes that are much more complex than the previous ones. This topic is very important for musical synthesis applications, but is outside of the scope of this book.

CHAPTER 5

Analysis and Visualization

So far we've only talked about audio synthesis and processing, but that is only half of the functionality that the Web Audio API provides. The other half, audio analysis, is all about understanding what the sound that is being played is like. The canonical example of this feature is visualization, but there are many other applications far outside the scope of this book, including pitch detection, rhythm detection, and speech recognition.

This is an important topic for us as game developers and interactive application builders for a couple of reasons. Firstly, a good visual analyzer can act as a sort of debugging tool (obviously in addition to your ears and a good metering setup) for tweaking sounds to be just right. Secondly, visualization is critical for any games and applications related to music, from games like *Guitar Hero* to software like GarageBand.

Frequency Analysis

The main way of doing sound analysis with the Web Audio API is to use `AnalyserNo des`. These nodes do not change the sound in any way, and can be placed anywhere in your audio context. Once this node is in your graph, it provides two main ways for you to inspect the sound wave: over the time domain and over the frequency domain.

The results you get are based on FFT analysis over a certain buffer size. We have a few knobs to customize the output of the node:

fftSize
> This defines the buffer size that is used to perform the analysis. It must be a power of two. Higher values will result in more fine-grained analysis of the signal, at the cost of some performance loss.

frequencyBinCount
> This is a read-only property, set automatically as fftSize/2.

`smoothingTimeConstant`
> This is a value between zero and one. A value of one causes a large moving average window and smoothed results. A value of zero means no moving average, and quickly fluctuating results.

The basic setup is to insert the analyzer node into the interesting part of our audio graph:

```
// Assume that node A is ordinarily connected to B.
var analyser = context.createAnalyser();
A.connect(analyser);
analyser.connect(B);
```

Then we can get frequency or time domain arrays as follows:

```
var freqDomain = new Float32Array(analyser.frequencyBinCount);
analyser.getFloatFrequencyData(freqDomain);
```

In the previous example, `freqDomain` is an array of 32-bit floats corresponding to the frequency domain. These values are normalized to be between zero and one. The indexes of the output can be mapped linearly between zero and the *nyquist frequency*, which is defined to be half of the sampling rate (available in the Web Audio API via `context.sampleRate`). The following snippet maps from frequency to the correct bucket in the array of frequencies:

```
function getFrequencyValue(frequency) {
  var nyquist = context.sampleRate/2;
  var index = Math.round(frequency/nyquist * freqDomain.length);
  return freqDomain[index];
}
```

If we are analyzing a 1,000-Hz sine wave, for example, we would expect that `getFrequencyValue(1000)` would return a peak value in the graph, as shown in Figure 5-1.

The frequency domain is also available in 8-bit unsigned units via the `getByteFrequencyData` call. The values of these integers is scaled to fit between `minDecibels` and `maxDecibels` (in dBFS) properties on the analyzer node, so these parameters can be tweaked to scale the output as desired.

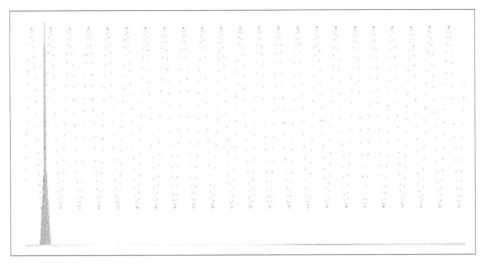

Figure 5-1. A 1,000-Hz tone being visualized (the full domain extends from 0 to 22,050 Hz)

Animating with requestAnimationFrame

If we want to build a visualization for our soundform, we need to periodically query the analyzer, process the results, and render them. We can do this by setting up a JavaScript timer like `setInterval` or `setTimeout`, but there's a better way: `requestAnimation Frame`. This API lets the browser incorporate your custom draw function into its native rendering loop, which is a great performance improvement. Instead of forcing it to draw at specific intervals and contending with the rest of the things a browser does, you just request it to be placed in the queue, and the browser will get to it as quickly as it can.

Because the `requestAnimationFrame` API is still experimental, we need to use the prefixed version depending on user agent, and fall back to a rough equivalent: `setTime out`. The code for this is as follows:

```
window.requestAnimationFrame = (function(){
return window.requestAnimationFrame    ||
  window.webkitRequestAnimationFrame  ||
  window.mozRequestAnimationFrame     ||
  window.oRequestAnimationFrame       ||
  window.msRequestAnimationFrame      ||
  function(callback){
  window.setTimeout(callback, 1000 / 60);
};
})();
```

Once we have this `requestAnimationFrame` function defined, we should use it to query the analyzer node to give us detailed information about the state of the audio stream.

Visualizing Sound

Putting it all together, we can set up a render loop that queries and renders the analyzer for its current frequency analysis as before, into a `freqDomain` array:

```
var freqDomain = new Uint8Array(analyser.frequencyBinCount);
analyser.getByteFrequencyData(freqDomain);
for (var i = 0; i < analyser.frequencyBinCount; i++) {
  var value = freqDomain[i];
  var percent = value / 256;
  var height = HEIGHT * percent;
  var offset = HEIGHT - height - 1;
  var barWidth = WIDTH/analyser.frequencyBinCount;
  var hue = i/analyser.frequencyBinCount * 360;
  drawContext.fillStyle = 'hsl(' + hue + ', 100%, 50%)';
  drawContext.fillRect(i * barWidth, offset, barWidth, height);
}
```

We can do a similar thing for the time-domain data as well:

```
var timeDomain = new Uint8Array(analyser.frequencyBinCount);
analyser.getByteTimeDomainData(freqDomain);
for (var i = 0; i < analyser.frequencyBinCount; i++) {
  var value = timeDomain[i];
  var percent = value / 256;
  var height = HEIGHT * percent;
  var offset = HEIGHT - height - 1;
  var barWidth = WIDTH/analyser.frequencyBinCount;
  drawContext.fillStyle = 'black';
  drawContext.fillRect(i * barWidth, offset, 1, 1);
}
```

This code plots time-domain values using HTML5 canvas, creating a simple visualizer that renders a graph of the waveform on top of the colorful bar graph, which represents frequency-domain data. The result is a canvas output that looks like Figure 5-2, and changes with time.

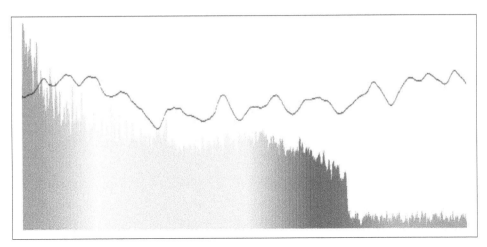

Figure 5-2. A screenshot of a visualizer in action

Demo: to see the above visualizer live, visit http://webaudioapi.com/samples/visualizer/.

Our approach to visualization misses a lot of data. For music visualization purposes, that's fine. If, however, we want to perform a comprehensive analysis of the whole audio buffer, we should look to other methods.

CHAPTER 6

Advanced Topics

This chapter covers topics that are very important, but slightly more complex than the rest of the book. We will dive into adding effects to sounds, generating synthetic sound effects without any audio buffers at all, simulating effects of different acoustic environments, and spatializing sound in 3D space.

CRITICAL THEORY
Biquad Filters

A filter can emphasize or de-emphasize certain parts of the frequency spectrum of a sound. Visually, it can be shown as a graph over the frequency domain called a *frequency response graph* (see Figure 6-1). For each frequency, the higher the value of the graph, the more emphasis is placed on that part of the frequency range. A graph sloping downward places more emphasis on low frequencies and less on high frequencies.

Web Audio filters can be configured with three parameters: gain, frequency, and a quality factor (also known as Q). These parameters all affect the frequency response graph differently.

There are many kinds of filters that can be used to achieve certain kinds of effects:

Low-pass filter
> Makes sounds more muffled

High-pass filter
> Makes sounds more tinny

Band-pass filter
> Cuts off lows and highs (e.g., telephone filter)

Low-shelf filter
> Affects the amount of bass in a sound (like the bass knob on a stereo)

High-shelf filter
  Affects the amount of treble in a sound (like the treble knob on a stereo)

Peaking filter
  Affects the amount of midrange in a sound (like the mid knob on a stereo)

Notch filter
  Removes unwanted sounds in a narrow frequency range

All-pass filter
  Creates phaser effects

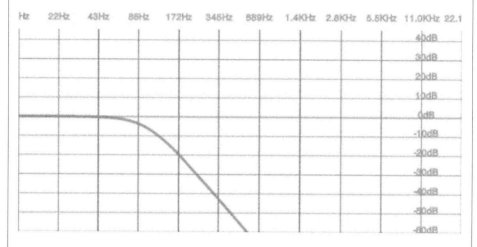

Figure 6-1. Frequency response graph for a low-pass filter

All of these biquad filters stem from a common mathematical model and can all be graphed like the low-pass filter in Figure 6-1. More details about these filters can be found in more mathematically demanding books such as *Real Sound Synthesis for Interactive Applications* by Perry R. Cook (A K Peters, 2002), which I highly recommend reading if you are interested in audio fundamentals.

Adding Effects via Filters

Using the Web Audio API, we can apply the filters discussed above using `BiquadFil terNodes`. This type of audio node is very commonly used to build equalizers and manipulate sounds in interesting ways. Let's set up a simple low-pass filter to eliminate low frequency noise from a sound sample:

```
// Create a filter
var filter = context.createBiquadFilter();
// Note: the Web Audio spec is moving from constants to strings.
// filter.type = 'lowpass';
filter.type = filter.LOWPASS;
filter.frequency.value = 100;
// Connect the source to it, and the filter to the destination.
```

Demo: to listen to a filter effect, visit http://webaudioapi.com/samples/filter/.

The BiquadFilterNode has support for all of the commonly used second-order filter types. We can configure these nodes with the same parameters as discussed in the previous section, and also visualize the frequency response graphs by using the getFrequencyResponse method on the node. Given an array of frequencies, this function returns an array of magnitudes of responses corresponding to each frequency.

Chris Wilson and Chris Rogers put together a great visualizer sample (Figure 6-2) that shows the frequency responses of all of the filter types available in the Web Audio API.

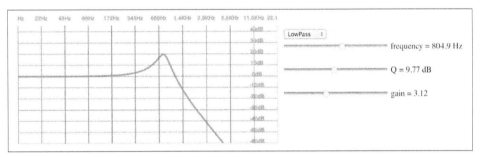

Figure 6-2. A graph of the frequency response of a low-pass filter with parameters

Demo: to plot frequency responses for various filter configurations using this tool, visit http://webaudioapi.com/samples/frequency-response/.

Procedurally Generated Sound

Up to now, we have been assuming that your game's sound sources are static. An audio designer creates a bunch of assets and hands them over to you. Then, you play them back with some parameterization depending on local conditions (for example, the room ambiance and relative positions of sources and listeners). This approach has a few disadvantages:

1. Sound assets will be very large. This is especially bad on the Web, where instead of loading from a hard drive, you load from a network (at least the first time), which is roughly an order of magnitude slower.

2. Even with many assets and tweaks to each, there is limited variety.

3. You need to find assets by scouring sound effects libraries, and then maybe worry about royalties. Plus, chances are, any given sound effect is already being used in other applications, so your users have unintended associations.

We can use the Web Audio API to fully generate sound procedurally. For example, let's simulate a gun firing. We begin with a buffer of white noise, which we can generate with a `ScriptProcessorNode` as follows:

```
function WhiteNoiseScript() {
  this.node = context.createScriptProcessor(1024, 1, 2);
  this.node.onaudioprocess = this.process;
}

WhiteNoiseScript.prototype.process = function(e) {
  var L = e.outputBuffer.getChannelData(0);
  var R = e.outputBuffer.getChannelData(1);
  for (var i = 0; i < L.length; i++) {
    L[i] = ((Math.random() * 2) - 1);
    R[i] = L[i];
  }
};
```

For more information on `ScriptProcessorNodes`, see "Audio Processing with Java-Script" (page 51).

This code is not an efficient implementation because JavaScript is required to constantly and dynamically create a stream of white noise. To increase efficiency, we can programmatically generate a mono `AudioBuffer` of white noise as follows:

```
function WhiteNoiseGenerated(callback) {
  // Generate a 5 second white noise buffer.
  var lengthInSamples = 5 * context.sampleRate;
  var buffer = context.createBuffer(1, lengthInSamples, context.sampleRate);
  var data = buffer.getChannelData(0);

  for (var i = 0; i < lengthInSamples; i++) {
    data[i] = ((Math.random() * 2) - 1);
  }

  // Create a source node from the buffer.
  this.node = context.createBufferSource();
  this.node.buffer = buffer;
  this.node.loop = true;
  this.node.start(0);
}
```

Next, we can simulate various phases of the gun firing—attack, decay, and release—in an envelope:

```
function Envelope() {
  this.node = context.createGain()
  this.node.gain.value = 0;
```

```
    }

    Envelope.prototype.addEventToQueue = function() {
      this.node.gain.linearRampToValueAtTime(0, context.currentTime);
      this.node.gain.linearRampToValueAtTime(1, context.currentTime + 0.001);
      this.node.gain.linearRampToValueAtTime(0.3, context.currentTime + 0.101);
      this.node.gain.linearRampToValueAtTime(0, context.currentTime + 0.500);
    };
```

Finally, we can connect the voice outputs to a filter to allow a simulation of distance:

```
    this.voices = [];
    this.voiceIndex = 0;

    var noise = new WhiteNoise();

    var filter = context.createBiquadFilter();
    filter.type = 0;
    filter.Q.value = 1;
    filter.frequency.value = 800;

    // Initialize multiple voices.
    for (var i = 0; i < VOICE_COUNT; i++) {
      var voice = new Envelope();
      noise.connect(voice.node);
      voice.connect(filter);
      this.voices.push(voice);
    }

    var gainMaster = context.createGainNode();
    gainMaster.gain.value = 5;
    filter.connect(gainMaster);

    gainMaster.connect(context.destination);
```

This example is borrowed from BBC's gunfire effects page (*http://webaudio.prototyp ing.bbc.co.uk/gunfire/*) with small modifications, including a port to JavaScript.

Demo: to hear a procedural gunshot effect, visit http://webaudioapi.com/samples/proce dural/.

As you can see, this approach is very powerful but gets complicated pretty quickly, going beyond the scope of this book. For more information about procedural sound generation, take a look at Andy Farnell's Practical Synthetic Sound Design (*http://obiwan nabe.co.uk/tutorials/html/tutorials_main.html*) tutorials and book.

Room Effects

Before sound gets from its source to our ears, it bounces off walls, buildings, furniture, carpets, and other objects. Every such collision changes properties of the sound. For example, clapping your hands outside sounds very different from clapping your hands inside a large cathedral, which can cause audible reverberations for several seconds. Games with high production value aim to imitate these effects. Creating a separate set of samples for each acoustic environment is often prohibitively expensive, since it requires a lot of effort from the audio designer, and a lot of assets, and thus a larger amount of game data.

The Web Audio API comes with a facility to simulate these various acoustic environments called a `ConvolverNode`. Examples of effects that you can get out of the convolution engine include chorus effects, reverberation, and telephone-like speech.

The idea for producing room effects is to play back a reference sound in a room, record it, and then (metaphorically) take the difference between the original sound and the recorded one. The result of this is an impulse response that captures the effect that the room has on a sound. These impulse responses are painstakingly recorded in very specific studio settings, and doing this on your own requires serious dedication. Luckily, there are sites that host many of these pre-recorded impulse response files (stored as audio files) for your convenience.

The Web Audio API provides an easy way to apply these impulse responses to your sounds using the `ConvolverNode`. This node takes an impulse response buffer, which is a regular `AudioBuffer` with the impulse response file loaded into it. The convolver is effectively a very complex filter (like the `BiquadFilterNode`), but rather than selecting from a set of effect types, it can be configured with an arbitrary filter response:

```
var impulseResponseBuffer = null;
function loadImpulseResponse() {
  loadBuffer('impulse.wav', function(buffer) {
    impulseResponseBuffer = buffer;
  });
}

function play() {
  // Make a source node for the sample.
  var source = context.createBufferSource();
  source.buffer = this.buffer;
  // Make a convolver node for the impulse response.
  var convolver = context.createConvolver();
  // Set the impulse response buffer.
  convolver.buffer = impulseResponseBuffer;
  // Connect graph.
  source.connect(convolver);
  convolver.connect(context.destination);
}
```

The convolver node "smushes" the input sound and its impulse response by computing a convolution, a mathematically intensive function. The result is something that sounds as if it was produced in the room where the impulse response was recorded. In practice, it often makes sense to mix the original sound (called the *dry mix*) with the convolved sound (called the *wet mix*), and use an equal-power crossfade to control how much of the effect you want to apply.

It's also possible to generate these impulse responses synthetically, but this topic is outside of the scope of this book.

Demo: to toggle between multiple room effects, visit http://webaudioapi.com/samples/ room-effects/.

Spatialized Sound

Games are often set in a world where objects have positions in space, either in 2D or in 3D. If this is the case, spatialized audio can greatly increase the immersiveness of the experience. Luckily, the Web Audio API comes with built-in positional audio features (stereo for now) that are quite straightforward to use.

As you experiment with spatialized sound (*http://connect.creativelabs.com/openal/ default.aspx*), make sure that you are listening through stereo speakers (preferably headphones). This will give you a better idea of how the left and right channels are being transformed by your spatialization approach.

The Web Audio API model has three aspects of increasing complexity, with many concepts borrowed from OpenAL:

1. Position and orientation of sources and listeners
2. Parameters associated with the source audio cones
3. Relative velocities of sources and listeners

There is a single listener (`AudioListener`) attached to the Web Audio API context that can be configured in space through position and orientation. Each source can be passed through a panner node (`AudioPannerNode`), which spatializes the input audio. Based on the relative position of the sources and the listener, the Web Audio API computes the correct gain modifications.

There are a few things to know about the assumptions that the API makes. The first is that the listener is at the origin $(0, 0, 0)$ by default. Positional API coordinates are unitless, so in practice, it takes some multiplier tweaking to make things sound the way you want. Secondly, orientations are specified as direction vectors (with a length of one). Finally, in this coordinate space, positive y points upward, which is the opposite of most computer graphics systems.

With these things in mind, here's an example of how you can change the position of a source node that is being spatialized in 2D via a panner node (`PannerNode`):

```
// Position the listener at the origin (the default, just added for the sake of
being explicit)
```

```
context.listener.setPosition(0, 0, 0);

// Position the panner node.
// Assume X and Y are in screen coordinates and the listener is at screen cen-
ter.
var panner = context.createPanner();
var centerX = WIDTH/2;
var centerY = HEIGHT/2;
var x = (X - centerX)  / WIDTH;
// The y coordinate is flipped to match the canvas coordinate space.
var y = (Y - centerY) / HEIGHT;
// Place the z coordinate slightly in behind the listener.
var z = -0.5;
// Tweak multiplier as necessary.
var scaleFactor = 2;
panner.setPosition(x * scaleFactor, y * scaleFactor, z);

// Convert angle into a unit vector.
panner.setOrientation(Math.cos(angle), -Math.sin(angle), 1);

// Connect the node you want to spatialize to a panner.
source.connect(panner);
```

In addition to taking into account relative positions and orientations, each source has a configurable audio cone, as shown in Figure 6-3.

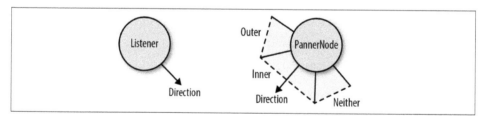

Figure 6-3. A diagram of panners and the listener in 2D space

Once you have specified an inner and outer cone, you end up with a separation of space into three parts, as seen in Figure 6-3:

1. Inner cone

2. Outer cone

3. Neither cone

Each of these sub-spaces can have a gain multiplier associated with it as an extra hint for the positional model. For example, to emulate targeted sound, we might have the following configuration:

```
panner.coneInnerAngle = 5;
panner.coneOuterAngle = 10;
```

```
panner.coneGain = 0.5;
panner.coneOuterGain = 0.2;
```

A dispersed sound can have a very different set of parameters. An omnidirectional source has a 360-degree inner cone, and its orientation makes no difference for spatialization:

```
panner.coneInnerAngle = 180;
panner.coneGain = 0.5;
```

In addition to position, orientation, and sound cones, sources and listeners can also specify velocity. This value is important for simulating pitch changes as a result of the doppler effect.

Demo: to experiment with 2D spatialized sound, visit http://webaudioapi.com/samples/ spatialized/.

Audio Processing with JavaScript

Generally speaking, the Web Audio API aims to provide enough primitives (mostly via audio nodes) to do most common audio tasks. The idea is that these modules are written in C++ and are much faster than the same code written in JavaScript.

However, the API also provides a ScriptProcessorNode that lets web developers synthesize and process audio directly in JavaScript. For example, you could prototype custom DSP effects using this approach, or illustrate concepts for educational applications.

To get started, create a ScriptProcessorNode. This node processes sound in chunks specified as a parameter to the node (bufferSize), which must be a power of two. Err on the side of using a larger buffer, since it gives you more of a safety margin against glitches if the main thread is busy with other things, such as page re-layout, garbage collection, or JavaScript callbacks:

```
// Create a ScriptProcessorNode.
var processor = context.createScriptProcessor(2048);
// Assign the onProcess function to be called for every buffer.
processor.onaudioprocess = onProcess;
// Assuming source exists, connect it to a script processor.
source.connect(processor);
```

Once you have the audio data piping into a JavaScript function, you can analyze the stream by examining the input buffer, or directly change the output by modifying the output buffer. For example, we can easily swap the left and right channels by implementing the following script processor:

```
function onProcess(e) {
  var leftIn = e.inputBuffer.getChannelData(0);
  var rightIn = e.inputBuffer.getChannelData(1);
  var leftOut = e.outputBuffer.getChannelData(0);
  var rightOut = e.outputBuffer.getChannelData(1);
```

```
  for (var i = 0; i < leftIn.length; i++) {
    // Flip left and right channels.
    leftOut[i] = rightIn[i];
    rightOut[i] = leftIn[i];
  }
}
```

Note that you should never do this channel swap in production, since using a Chan
nelSplitterNode followed by a ChannelMergerNode is far more efficient. As another
example, we can add a random noise to the mix. We do this by simply adding a random
offset to the signal. By making the signal completely random, we can generate white
noise, which is actually quite useful in many applications [see "Procedurally Generated
Sound" (page 45)]:

```
function onProcess(e) {
  var leftOut = e.outputBuffer.getChannelData(0);
  var rightOut = e.outputBuffer.getChannelData(1);

  for (var i = 0; i < leftOut.length; i++) {
    // Add some noise
    leftOut[i] += (Math.random() - 0.5) * NOISE_FACTOR;
    rightOut[i] += (Math.random() - 0.5) * NOISE_FACTOR;
  }
}
```

The main issue with using script processing nodes is performance. Using JavaScript to
implement these mathematically-intensive algorithms is significantly slower than implementing them directly in the native code of the browser.

*Demo: for a full example of script processor nodes, visit http://webaudioapi.com/samples/
script-processor/.*

CHAPTER 7

Integrating with Other Technologies

The Web Audio API makes audio processing and analysis a fundamental part of the web platform. As a core building block for web developers, it is designed to play well with other technologies.

Setting Up Background Music with the <audio> Tag

As I mentioned at the very start of the book, the <audio> tag has many limitations that make it undesirable for games and interactive applications. One advantage of this HTML5 feature, however, is that it has built-in buffering and streaming support, making it ideal for long-form playback. Loading a large buffer is slow from a network perspective, and expensive from a memory-management perspective. The <audio> tag setup is ideal for music playback or for a game soundtrack.

Rather than going the usual path of loading a sound directly by issuing an XMLHttpRequest and then decoding the buffer, you can use the media stream audio source node (MediaElementAudioSourceNode) to create nodes that behave much like audio source nodes (AudioSourceNode), but wrap an existing <audio> tag. Once we have this node connected to our audio graph, we can use our knowledge of the Web Audio API to do great things. This small example applies a low-pass filter to the <audio> tag:

```
window.addEventListener('load', onLoad, false);

function onLoad() {
  var audio = new Audio();
  source = context.createMediaElementSource(audio);
  var filter = context.createBiquadFilter();
  filter.type = filter.LOWPASS;
  filter.frequency.value = 440;

  source.connect(this.filter);
  filter.connect(context.destination);
```

```
    audio.src = 'http://example.com/the.mp3';
    audio.play();
}
```

Demo: to see <audio> *tag integration with the Web Audio API in action, visit http://webaudioapi.com/samples/audio-tag/.*

Live Audio Input

One highly requested feature of the Web Audio API is integration with getUserMedia, which gives browsers access to the audio/video stream of connected microphones and cameras. At the time of this writing, this feature is available behind a flag in Chrome. To enable it, you need to visit about:flags and turn on the "Web Audio Input" experiment, as in Figure 7-1.

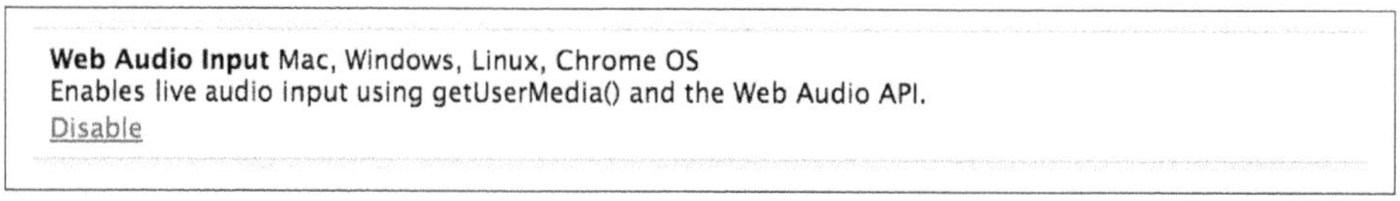

Web Audio Input Mac, Windows, Linux, Chrome OS
Enables live audio input using getUserMedia() and the Web Audio API.
Disable

Figure 7-1. Enabling web audio input in Chrome

Once this is enabled, you can use the MediaStreamSourceNode Web Audio node. This node wraps around the audio stream object that is available once the stream is established. This is directly analogous to the way that MediaElementSourceNodes wrap <audio> elements. In the following sample, we visualize the live audio input that has been processed by a notch filter:

```
function getLiveInput() {
  // Only get the audio stream.
  navigator.webkitGetUserMedia({audio: true}, onStream, onStreamError);
};

function onStream(stream) {
  // Wrap a MediaStreamSourceNode around the live input stream.
  var input = context.createMediaStreamSource(stream);
  // Connect the input to a filter.
  var filter = context.createBiquadFilter();
  filter.frequency.value = 60.0;
  filter.type = filter.NOTCH;
  filter.Q = 10.0;

  var analyser = context.createAnalyser();

  // Connect graph.
  input.connect(filter);
  filter.connect(analyser);
```

```
  // Set up an animation.
  requestAnimationFrame(render);
};

function onStreamError(e) {
  console.error(e);
};

function render() {
  // Visualize the live audio input.
  requestAnimationFrame(render);
};
```

Another way to establish streams is based on a WebRTC PeerConnection. By bringing a communication stream into the Web Audio API, you could, for example, spatialize multiple participants in a video conference.

Demo: to visualize live input, visit http://webaudioapi.com/samples/microphone/.

Page Visibility and Audio Playback

Whenever you develop a web application that involves audio playback, you should be cognizant of the state of the page. The classic failure mode here is that one of many tabs is playing sound, but you have no idea which one it is. This may make sense for a music player application, in which you want music to continue playing regardless of the visibility of the page. However, for a game, you often want to pause gameplay (and sound playback) when the page is no longer in the foreground.

Luckily, the Page Visibility API provides functionality to detect when a page becomes hidden or visible. The state can be determined from the Boolean `document.hidden` property. The event that fires when the visibility changes is called `visibilitychange`. Because the API is still considered to be experimental, all of these names are webkit-prefixed. With this in mind, the following code will stop a source node when a page becomes hidden, and resume it when the page becomes visible:

```
// Listen to the webkitvisibilitychange event.
document.addEventListener('webkitvisibilitychange', onVisibilityChange);

function onVisibilityChange() {
  if (document.webkitHidden) {
    source.stop(0);
  } else {
    source.start(0);
  }
}
```

CHAPTER 8

Conclusion

Thanks for reading this book on the Web Audio API. If you are a digital-audio novice, I hope that I have succeeded in giving you a solid understanding of some of the fundamental concepts. If you are a Web Audio API enthusiast, hopefully you learned something new.

Before closing, I would like to point you to a number of excellent books and web resources that I found extremely interesting and useful while researching and writing this book. My top five follow:

1. The "Web Audio API Specification" (*https://dvcs.w3.org/hg/audio/raw-file/tip/webaudio/specification.html*) by Chris Rogers

2. *Real Sound Synthesis for Interactive Applications* by Perry R. Cook (A K Peters, 2002)

3. *Mastering Audio: The Art and the Science* by Bob Katz (Focal Press, 2002)

4. Andy Farnell's "Practical Synthetic Sound Design" (*http://obiwannabe.co.uk/tutorials/html/tutorials_main.html*) tutorials

5. "All About Decibels, Part I: What's your dB IQ?" (*http://faculty.mccneb.edu/ccarlson/VACA1010/VACA1010_CD/dB%20part%201.pdf*) by Lionel Dumond

Deprecation Notes

The Web Audio API is still evolving, and some methods are being added, removed, and renamed. This section describes some of the recent changes made to the API:

- `AudioBufferSourceNode.noteOn()` has been changed to `start()`.
- `AudioBufferSourceNode.noteGrainOn()` has been changed to `start()`.
- `AudioBufferSourceNode.noteOff()` has been changed to `stop()`.
- `AudioContext.createGainNode()` has been changed to `createGain()`.
- `AudioContext.createDelayNode()` has been changed to `createDelay()`.
- `AudioContext.createJavaScriptNode()` has been changed to `createScriptProcessor()`.
- `OscillatorNode.noteOn()` has been changed to `start()`.
- `OscillatorNode.noteOff()` has been changed to `stop()`.
- `AudioParam.setTargetValueAtTime()` has been changed to `setTargetAtTime()`.

In addition to these changes, many of the constants in the Web Audio API are changing from variables into string enumerations. For example, filter types are going from `filter.LOWPASS` to `lowpass`, oscillator types are going from `osc.SINE` to `sine`, etc.

Throughout the book, I've used new versions of all of the APIs, so those using older implementations of the API may need to revert back to earlier methods and constant naming.

For the most up-to-date information regarding naming changes, see the Web Audio specification (*http://bit.ly/105wGL0*).

Glossary

Audio context
A container for all audio nodes in the Web Audio API graph.

Bit depth
The number of bits allocated for each value in an audio data stream.

Bit rate
The number of bits per second that a compressed audio file will output.

Cents
A logarithmic unit of measure used for musical intervals. Twelve-tone equal temperament divides the octave into 12 semitones of 100 cents each.

Clipping
What happens to an audio wave when it exceeds the highest permitted value (0 dBFS).

Decibels
A relative unit used to measure the intensity of a sound signal.

dBFS
Sound level relative to the full scale (nominally 0 dBFS). This unit is negative unless sound is being clipped.

dBSPL
Sound pressure level relative to the threshold of human hearing.

FFT
Fast Fourier Transform, an algorithm for breaking a sound wave up into its constituent sine waves.

Hertz
A measure of frequency. The number of times per second that something happens.

Nyquist frequency
    Half of the sample rate of an audio buffer.

PCM
    Pulse code modulation, a way of storing sound waves as an array of numbers.

Playback rate
    The speed at which an audio buffer is played back.

Sample rate
    The number of times per second that an analog sound is sampled during quantization, or the process of converting an analog signal into a digital one.

About the Author

Boris Smus is a frontend engineer working for Google Chrome developer relations, specializing in mobile web and web audio. Before joining Google, he worked as a human –computer interaction researcher at Carnegie Mellon and as a software engineer at Apple.

Colophon

The animal on the cover of *Web Audio API* is a brown long-eared bat (*Plecotus auritus*).

The cover image is from Cassell's *Natural History*. The cover font is Adobe ITC Garamond. The text font is Adobe Minion Pro; the heading font is Adobe Myriad Condensed; and the code font is Dalton Maag's Ubuntu Mono.

Have it your way.

Get even more for your money.

Join the O'Reilly Community, and register the O'Reilly books you own. It's free, and you'll get:

- $4.99 ebook upgrade offer
- 40% upgrade offer on O'Reilly print books
- Membership discounts on books and events
- Free lifetime updates to ebooks and videos
- Multiple ebook formats, DRM FREE
- Participation in the O'Reilly community
- Newsletters
- Account management
- 100% Satisfaction Guarantee

Signing up is easy:

1. **Go to: oreilly.com/go/register**
2. **Create an O'Reilly login.**
3. **Provide your address.**
4. **Register your books.**

Note: English-language books only

To order books online:
oreilly.com/store

For questions about products or an order:
orders@oreilly.com

To sign up to get topic-specific email announcements and/or news about upcoming books, conferences, special offers, and new technologies:
elists@oreilly.com

For technical questions about book content:
booktech@oreilly.com

To submit new book proposals to our editors:
proposals@oreilly.com

O'Reilly books are available in multiple DRM-free ebook formats. For more information:
oreilly.com/ebooks

Spreading the knowledge of innovators   oreilly.com

Milton Keynes UK
Ingram Content Group UK Ltd.
UKHW051008131024
449552UK00007B/130